CONFUCIUS

教师

CONFUCIUS

Philosopher and Teacher
by Josh Wilker

A Book Report Biography
FRANKLIN WATTS
A Division of Grolier Publishing
New York / London / Hong Kong / Sydney
Danbury, Connecticut

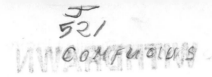

521

For my father, Louis Wilker, and for Morton Gaber, Ngai Chan, Dave Gantz, Larry Cafaro, Neil Shepard, and Tony Whedon.

frontispiece: This portrait of Confucius is based on the traditional conception of his appearance.

Cover illustration by Kinuko Y. Craft

Map by XNR Productions.

Photographs ©: AP/Wide World Photos: 58, 70, 97; Art Resource: 38 (Giraudon), 16 (Erich Lessing), 23 (Nimatallah), 81 (Vanni), 19, 86 (Werner Forman Archive); Bridgeman Art Library International Ltd., London/New York: 93 ("Reporting our harvest to Chairman Mao", propaganda poster from the Chinese Cultural Revolution.1966-76 by Chinese School (20th century) Private Collection); Corbis-Bettmann: 2, 12, 28, 37, 46, 53, 77; Library of Congress: 40; Network Aspen: 95 (Jeffrey Aaronson); New York Public Library Picture Collection: 32; Reuters/Corbis-Bettmann: 91; UPI/Corbis-Bettmann: 65, 72.

Visit Franklin Watts on the Internet at:
http://publishing.grolier.com

Library of Congress Cataloging-in-Publication Data

Wilker, Josh.
    Confucius: philosopher and teacher / Josh Wilker
      p. cm. — (A book report biography)
    Includes bibliographical references and index.
    Summary: A biography of the Chinese teacher and sage whose teachings influenced all aspects of Chinese life for many centuries after his death.
    ISBN 0-531-11436-8
    1.Confucius—Juvenile literature 2.Philosophers—China–Biography—Juvenile literature. [1. Confucius. 2. Philosophers.] I. Title. II. Series.
B128.C8W58 1998
181'.112—dc21
[B]   97-18362
                                        CIP
                                        AC

GROLIER
PUBLISHING

CONTENTS

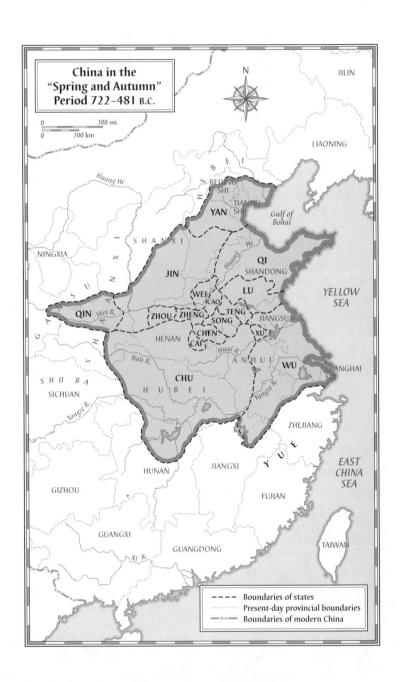

China in the
"Spring and Autumn"
Period 722–481 B.C.

0   200 mi.
0   200 km

JILIN

LIAONING

Huang He

H E B E I

BEIJING SHI

TIANJIN SHI

YAN

Gulf of Bohai

S H A N X I

NINGXIA

G A N S U

S H A A N X I

JIN

Huang He

QI

SHANDONG

YELLOW SEA

WEI

CAO

LU

QIN

Wei R.

ZHOU

ZHENG

TENG

SONG

JIANGSU

CHEN

XU

HENAN

CAI

Huai R.

A N H U I

Han R.

WU

SHANGHAI SHI

SHU

BA

SICHUAN

CHU

H U B E I

Yangze R.

Yangze R.

ZHEJIANG

EAST CHINA SEA

HUNAN

JIANGXI

Y U E

GIZHOU

FUJIAN

GUANGXI

GUANGDONG

Xi R.

TAIWAN

- - - - Boundaries of states
·········· Present-day provincial boundaries
-··-··- Boundaries of modern China

CHAPTER ONE

教师

HEAVEN'S WOODEN BELL

The border guard had grown old. By the turn of the fifth century B.C., he had been stationed at the boundary between the Chinese states of Lu and Wei for decades. He had watched the world around him fall farther and farther into ruin. The epoch known in Chinese history as the Spring and Autumn Period (770–481 B.C.) was near its end. The border guard watched the people of this deteriorating world pass him by. He felt more and more as if he had become the lone spectator at a sad and disturbing parade.

Foremost in the parade were the soldiers. Treaties that had in earlier times invoked the name of Heaven to help keep the peace between states were now routinely disregarded. Bloody conflicts raged in all corners of the land, driven by warlords hungry for wealth, land, and power. In the relatively peaceful days of the Western Zhou Dynasty (1027–771 B.C.), rulers followed a moral code called the Way of Heaven. The Way of Heaven's basic directive was that leaders should govern their states to promote the well-being of the entire population. But by the fifth century B.C., the Way of Heaven had been cast off and forgotten, trampled as if by the countless, ever-marching soldiers. "If we can gain advantage over our enemies," a leader from the state of Chu told his army in a statement typical of the times, "we must advance without consideration of covenants."

Also in this parade, in ever-increasing numbers, were masses of peasants migrating from one war-torn region to another. To the rulers of China, these peasants were nothing more than a natural resource. In times of war they were used as soldiers, and in all times they were to be heavily taxed. They passed through the old man's gate, looking used up and thrown away.

Closing the parade were those who had decided that the world would never be put right. They were quitting the world, giving it up, going to live out their days in the wilderness amongst the birds and the beasts. They saw the human world as forever lost in chaos. "The whole universe is swept along by the same flood," one of them said. "Who can reverse its flow?

DREAM OF A BETTER WORLD

A ragged caravan appeared on the horizon. The border guard saw they weren't soldiers. They carried no weapons. They carried little more than the clothes on their back, but they weren't peasants either. They didn't look used up and thrown away.

As the caravan drew nearer, the border guard focused on the man who appeared to be the leader. He was the oldest of the group, and he seemed both humble and unshakably proud. In later years, it would be written that this man "was affable yet stern; he had authority without being overbearing; he was dignified but easy to approach." He and his companions drew closer still, and the guard could see the man's eyes. They gleamed like the eyes of a curious child. This man was not part of the sad parade.

The caravan came to a stop in front of the border guard. The guard looked up at the man with the gleaming eyes. "Whenever a gentleman comes to these parts," the guard said, "I always ask to see him."

In the centuries that followed, the man standing before the border guard would prove to be one of the most important and influential figures in all of human history. Confucius—a Westernized version of the Chinese name Kong Fuzi ("Master Kong")—looms as large, historically speaking, as

This engraving shows Confucius (in wagon) leaving his homeland of Lu.

any person who has ever lived. His ideas first took hold in China and then swept through the countries surrounding China, shaping the political, religious, and social makeup of the entire Far East. At the time he sat down in private to exchange ideas with the old border guard, however, Confucius was not an imposing figure at all. In the eyes of the world, he was a failure.

Early on in his life, Confucius had come to believe that the only truly joyous way for a person to live was with a strong interest in the welfare of others. He once said to one of his disciples, "As for the good man: what he wishes to achieve for himself, he helps others to achieve; what he wishes to obtain for himself, he enables others to attain."

With this thought in mind, he had set out from a young age to obtain an influential job in government. He believed that a government's only aim should be to secure and promote the welfare of the people. This was a radical idea in his day. The only thought in the minds of the rulers of China at that time was to get as rich and powerful as possible. They had little interest in a vision of a more humane, just, and harmonious world. They ignored Confucius, year after year, and finally, at the age of 50, Confucius left his home in hopes of finding someone in power to listen to his ideas. He was on his way out of Lu when the border guard asked to speak with him.

He had not set out on his journey alone. Myths and legends that arose after Confucius's death inflated into the thousands the number of men that followed him through China. Actually, only a handful of men were willing to accompany Confucius on his dangerous and far-fetched quest. Few could cut against the currents of the times, forsaking thoughts of personal security and wealth to follow what their teacher referred to as "The Way."

"In the morning follow the Way, in the evening die content," Confucius had told them. His disciples had originally come to him as they would have come to any tutor, hoping merely to learn the

> **"In the morning follow the Way, in the evening die content."**

skills needed to be a successful government worker. But Confucius had shared with them his dream of a better world and their hunger for personal success had been replaced by a wish to help build that world. They had come to share in Confucius's dream.

This dream seemed a long way off as they lingered on the boundary between Lu and Wei, waiting for Confucius to finish talking with the border guard. Much closer was the sting they felt at their master's utter failure to influence affairs in Lu.

Much closer, also, were worries about what lay ahead. They sensed that rulers in other parts of China would be just as greedy and immoral as the rulers of Lu. They saw failure in the past and failure in the future.

A VISION OF THE FUTURE

When the border guard emerged from his meeting with Confucius, he had a look on his face that the disciples recognized, for it was a look they themselves frequently wore after talking with Confucius. He looked, in a word, happy.

Confucius was a man who, in spite of his failures, enjoyed life immensely. Once, after hearing that a nobleman had asked one of his disciples about him, Confucius said, "Why didn't you say 'He is the sort of man who, in his enthusiasm for learning, forgets to eat, in his joy forgets to worry, and who ignores the approach of old age'?"

His passion to learn was contagious. It brought the dream of a better world closer. "Is goodness out of reach?" he once asked. "As soon as I long for goodness, goodness is at hand." The dream of a better world was no longer a distant illusion but became, through

"As soon as I long for goodness, goodness is at hand."

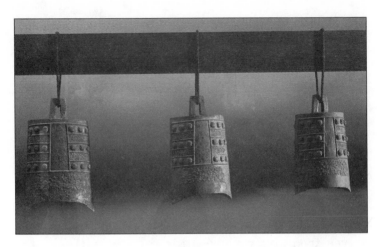

These bronze bells were made during the period 770–481 B.C. They are similar to the the wooden bell rung by the border guard.

Confucius, something as close at hand as a beautiful song. The old border guard, as he beamed at the disciples, seemed now to be hearing this song.

The border guard sensed what was weighing heavily on the disciples' minds. "Sirs, you must not be disheartened by his failure," he said. "It is now a very long while since the Way prevailed in the world."

The border guard wanted to communicate to the disciples the vision of the future that he had received while talking to Confucius. He had seen beyond the setbacks of one lifetime. He had seen a future where Confucius's ideas would be heard.

He picked up a wooden bell. It was the kind of wooden bell used at that time to herald news or to warn of approaching danger. He raised the wooden bell and began to rattle it. The disciples all looked up at him. The sound of the rattling bell filled the room, just as Confucius's ideas would soon enough fill the world. "Heaven will make use of your Master!" shouted the border guard, his eyes gleaming like the eyes of a child. "Heaven is going to use him as its wooden bell!"

CHAPTER TWO

教师

ONE WHO LOVES LEARNING

The man whose ideas would change the world came from humble beginnings. In a rare statement about his past, Confucius said simply, "In my youth, I was poor."

That statement comes from a slim collection of sayings and anecdotes called *The Analects of Confucius.* Compiled by some of his disciples not long after his death, *The Analects* serves as the most trustworthy source of information about the life of Confucius. It is for the most part free of the kind of myths and legends that later helped build Confucius into a near-godlike figure and thus obscure the actual facts of his life.

What little reliable information has come down through the centuries suggests that Confucius's father, a man named Kong Shuleang He, was a soldier or a minister in the service of the powerful Meng family. He was at least 70 years

According to legend, Confucius was born in
this cave in the Ni Mountains near Cou.

old at the time of Confucius's birth in 551 B.C. Whatever money or influence he had acquired through his position with the Meng family seems not to have been passed on to Confucius. It also seems certain that Shuleang He was not around to help raise Confucius.

The earliest biography of Confucius, written 350 years after his death by writer Sima Qian, depicts Confucius's birth in the town of Cou as the product of a "wild union." This term strongly suggests that his mother and father were never married.

There is no mention of Confucius's mother's family in any of the record books of the times. She came from the kind of family that record books never concerned themselves with—a peasant family. Her name was Yan Chengzai. No other reliable information about her exists.

What is known is that Confucius, later in life, would use the value of love and respect for one's parents as one of the cornerstones of his philosophy. He stressed that a person should care for and heed the wishes of his or her parents at all times, and that, more important, such behavior had to come straight from the heart. "Nowadays people think they are dutiful sons when they feed their parents. Yet they also feed their dogs and horses. Unless there is respect, where is the difference?"

"Unless there is respect, where is the difference?"

Confucius saw that it was in the family that a person first learned the necessity and the joy of sacrificing his or her own personal wishes for the good of others. It is possible that Confucius's first sight of this kind of heartfelt sacrifice came while watching his impoverished mother find a way to keep food on the table and a roof over their heads.

A THIRST FOR KNOWLEDGE

Later in life, Confucius stressed only one aspect of his childhood years — "At fifteen, I set my mind upon learning." At that time in Lu, youngsters were tutored by men either retired from, or still working in, the government. Children born of peasants were seldom given a chance to enter into study with these tutors. Confucius's father's position was probably what allowed him to begin his formal education.

As a youngster, Confucius displayed a passion for knowledge. He later regarded this passion as his one defining characteristic: "In a hamlet of ten houses, you will certainly find people as loyal and faithful as I, but you will not find one person who loves learning as much as I do."

For Confucius, the particulars of an education were never as important as the unquenchable thirst for knowledge with which that education was undertaken. When he later became a tutor himself, he told his disciples, "Learn as if you were following someone whom you could not catch up with, as though it were someone you were frightened of losing."

> **"Learn as if you were following someone whom you could not catch up with, as though it were someone you were frightened of losing."**

The tutors of that time taught fundamental skills such as reading, writing, and arithmetic. They often taught their students how to perform sacrificial rituals believed to be important in keeping the human world on good terms with the spirit world. The tutors also taught the conduct considered proper between people, an important skill for the students as they prepared for careers as advisors or ministers in the government. They needed to know the proper way to act in all the different situations that they would encounter as government officials.

▲ LONG HISTORY

During the first years of his education, Confucius undoubtedly became acquainted with China's extensive history. The civilization that he had been born into had existed for more than a thousand years. According to the legends of the time, China had been founded with the establishment of the Xia dynasty (ca. 2100–ca. 1600 B.C.) by the godlike rulers Yao, Shun, and Yu. Although there is no archaeological evidence to support the existence

This elephant-shaped container dates from the Shang dynasty (ca. 1700–1027 B.C.), the first Chinese dynasty known conclusively to have existed.

of this dynasty, archaeologists have found evidence to prove that the following dynasty, the Shang (ca. 1700–1027 B.C.), did exist. In 1027 B.C., the Zhou dynasty was established. Confucius focused much of his learning about the past on the early years of the Zhou dynasty.

CHINESE DYNASTIES

In China, a dynasty was a ruling family that held power for a fairly long time, usually for generations. With a few exceptions, China was ruled by a succession of dynasties for about four thousand years. Here are the major Chinese dynasties and their years of rule:

Xia	ca. 2100 B.C.–ca. 1600 B.C.
Shang	ca. 1700 B.C.–1027 B.C.
Zhou	1027 B.C.–256 B.C.
Qin	221 B.C.–206 B.C.
Han	206 B.C.–220 A.D.
Sui	589–618
Tang	618–907
Song	960–1279
Yuan	1279–1368
Ming	1368–1644
Qing	1644–1912

The Zhou rulers came to power by overthrowing a thoroughly corrupt Shang emperor. Such an act had previously been unthinkable because, no matter how bad a ruler's behavior became, he was considered holy. The emperor was a Son of Heaven, and he ruled by virtue of a Mandate of Heaven. To justify their seizure of power, the Zhou rulers had to find a way to make their takeover seem in accord with Heaven's will.

They did this by depicting themselves as being guided by Heaven in their takeover and charged to rule the land with the good will and sense of justice that Heaven intended for the people. Of vital importance to Confucius was that this set an example for rulers in China. The rulers now had to strive to be moral and good and had to concern themselves with the welfare of the people. Otherwise, their Mandate of Heaven would be revoked, and they would be overthrown.

Confucius looked around him as he studied the past. The current "Son of Heaven" had been reduced to a puppet emperor by powerful families throughout the land. These families paid no heed to Heaven's will and didn't care about the welfare of the people. The unwritten contract between the ruler and the people that was born when the Zhou leaders came to power simply didn't apply to these families, and they turned China into a bloody battleground.

In the early years of the Zhou dynasty, China was a unified and generally peaceful land, not a patchwork of battling states. Confucius would eventually hold up the founders the Zhou dynasty—King Wen, King Wu, and, especially, the Duke of Zhou—as ideals of virtue for the selfless way in which they governed China. A disciple of

Confucius's characterized his Master's education as a spirited search for "The Way" of these ancient, near-mythic figures, a search that extended beyond the lessons of any single tutor.

"The way of King Wen and King Wu . . . always remained alive among the people," said the disciple. "The wise retained its essentials, the ignorant retained a few details. All of them had some elements of the Way of King Wen and King Wu. There is no one from whom our Master could not have learned something; and there is no one who could have been our Master's exclusive teacher."

Confucius agreed, asserting that his education came from everywhere. He said, "Put me in the company of any two people at random—they will invariably have something to teach me. I can take their qualities as a model and their defects as a warning."

His fellow students focused on learning the skills necessary to find personal success in government. Confucius watched and learned from the entire world.

"Put me in the company of any two people at random—they will invariably have something to teach me."

CHAPTER THREE

教师

DREAMING OF THE DUKE OF ZHOU

In Qi, a state to the north of Lu, merchants got rich selling special footgear that accommodated the growing number of people who'd had their feet mutilated as a punishment. In the state of Jin, a ruler amused himself by going up into a tower and launching arrows at passersby. Another ruler routinely tested new swords on servants. Servants were also used widely to test their ruler's food for poison.

Soldiers marched throughout China, leaving rubble and wide-eyed corpses in their wake. In 593 B.C., the constant warfare took such a toll on the peasants of the state of Song that, to avoid starvation, they resorted to cannibalism.

It was a lawless, turbulent time, and Confucius's homeland of Lu was no exception. Much of the disorder and suffering there was caused by the rise to power of three ruthless families: the

This engraving shows Confucius instructing his students.

Meng, the Shu, and the Ji. In 609 B.C. these families conspired to murder two youthful heirs to the throne of Lu and installed a duke more willing to bend to their every wish. In 537 B.C., the year before a 15-year-old Confucius "set his mind on learning," the Ji family seized half the state. The Meng and the Shu split up the other half, and the Duke of Lu was left to survive on any contributions the three families saw fit to give him.

Throughout China, as the fortunes of aristocrats rose and fell, a new class gradually came into existence to join the huge, poverty-stricken peasant class and the small, rich ruling class. This third class, called in Chinese the SHI, was made up of people who were aristocrats in name only. They had descended from nobility, yet they found themselves with little, if any, land, wealth, or power of their own. Economically, they were seldom better off than the peasants. They were, with very few exceptions, a bitter, discontented, and highly ambitious lot. Their family name had afforded their ancestors a life of wealth and luxury, and they wanted that life, too. Now the only thing that their family name was good for was to open the doors to jobs serving those in power. The SHI served as soldiers, merchants, traders, advisors, or officers. Many set their mind on climbing to the top by way of whatever job they had, with little concern for whether their actions were right or wrong.

Confucius's father had been a member of this new class. Shuleang He's social standing would have passed down to his son had Confucius not been born out of wedlock and raised solely by his peasant mother. It was probably a little unclear just what social class Confucius belonged to when, in his early twenties, his mother died. At that time, Confucius found out where his father had been buried, and he buried his mother next to him. This act—which, according to many sources, cost Confucius much time, money, and effort—was most likely done out of sincere respect and love for his mother. It also clarified Confucius' social standing. By burying his mother alongside his father, he was publicly laying claim to the fact that he was his father's son. His father's name was his name. He was not a peasant but, like his father, a member of the SHI.

A JOB TO DO

Confucius got a job counting grain in the granary of the Ji family. It was not a particularly lofty start to a career that Confucius hoped would lead to a place at the side of a great ruler, but Confucius did not complain. "I was poor," he said, "therefore I had to become adept at a variety of lowly skills."

> **"I was poor, therefore I had to become adept at a variety of lowly skills."**

Confucius believed that everyone in a society has a role to play, and that role, whatever it is, should be played well. He didn't let his ambitious dreams interfere with the task at hand. "Confucius was once keeper of the stores [of grain]," wrote Confucius's greatest philosophical heir, Mencius, "and he said, 'It is only necessary that my accounts be correct. Mencius also wrote of Confucius's next job: "He was put in charge of pastures, and said, 'It is my duty only to see that the oxen and sheep are well-grown and strong.

Confucius's jobs allowed him occasionally to travel beyond the confines of his small hometown. He was able to meet people of many different walks of life and to learn from them. Also, as he began to travel to more populated areas, he was able to visit bigger libraries. He was able, for the first time, to get his hands on an ancient and voluminous anthology called the Book of Poems.

Confucius loved this book. Judging from the manner in which he spoke of the book later in his life, it must have seemed, when he first opened it up, to glow like moonlight in his hands. He soon came to view the Book of Poems as a vast series of gleaming signposts lighting up the virtuous Way of the ancients. In later years he would constantly urge his disciples to look to the poems for inspiration and for direction in their lives. To one disciple—his son, Boyu—he would say, "Whoever goes into life without having worked through the Poems will remain stuck, as if facing a wall."

Confucius believed that a single principle radiated through all of the poems. This principle alone had the power to shatter any wall. He said, "The three hundred Poems can be summed up in a single phrase: 'Think no evil.'

This portrait of Confucius is set in a library. Confucius's love of knowledge was stoked when he visited libraries as a young man.

THE DUKE OF ZHOU

From his earliest visits to the libraries, Confucius tried to embody this single principle. He also used the poems and the history books he found to fly back through time to the golden age of the Early Zhou dynasty. The books brought Confucius face to face with the Duke of Zhou. One poem read:

> *Broken were our axes*
>
> *And chipped were our hatchets.*
>
> *But since the Duke of Zhou*
> *came from the East*
>
> *Throughout the kingdom all is well.*

The Duke of Zhou cemented his place in history as a model of virtue when he neglected to seize power after the death of his brother King Wu. He instead acted as a regent for his young nephew King Cheng, concerning himself solely with the welfare of the government and the people it served. His wise and selfless leadership ushered in a period of great harmony in China and laid the cultural foundation for the longest-lasting dynasty in Chinese history.

The Duke of Zhou came to dominate Confucius's thoughts as a young man. He even began to dream about him. In his waking hours, Confucius looked around his world and saw moral corruption spreading across the land like a creeping vine. Above the cultural decay stood his image of the Duke of Zhou. Confucius believed it was possible to have a government that looked out for the welfare of its people. He believed that virtue could exist.

Confucius hoped that he might become a latter-day Duke of Zhou. But as a young man, he found it impossible to attain even the lowest position in government. He lacked the money and the noble family name that helped open doors of opportunity for his peers in the SHI class. Furthermore, his peasant upbringing left him with the kind of "rough edges" that have always been looked down upon by members of the upper class. Elegant speech did not flow from him as it did from the other SHI.

Confucius saw that these SHI spoke honeyed words merely for their own advancement. The advancement of the Way of the ancients, or of any kind of higher purpose at all, didn't matter to these men. "Clever talk and affected manners," Confucius observed, "are seldom signs of goodness."

Confucius never sweetened his words. This, more than anything else, crippled his chances of success in government. Instead of joining the other SHI in telling those in power exactly what they wanted to hear, Confucius chose to remain silent. And on those rare occasions when he did speak of the political leaders who might have aided his advancement, his words were like flying arrows whose tips had been dipped in acid. He was at one point asked to comment on the moral fiber of the current high-ranking government officials of Lu. "Pah!" he replied. "These puny creatures aren't even worth mentioning!"

"Clever talk and affected manners, are seldom signs of goodness."

CHAPTER FOUR

教师

JUNZI

In his mid-twenties, Confucius began to teach in Lu. He took to it like a young bird takes to flight. His own joy of learning soared into the greater joy of passing that learning on. He had been born to teach, just as he had been born to learn continually — "To store up knowledge in silence, to remain forever hungry for learning, to teach others without tiring — all this comes naturally to me."

He demanded of his students what he demanded of himself. This meant, first of all, that they had to be hungry for knowledge. He wasn't going to spoon feed them any answers. "Only one who bursts with eagerness do I instruct," he said. "Only one who bubbles with excitement, do I enlighten. If I uncover one corner and a student cannot discover the other three, I end the lesson."

Confucius began teaching when he was in his mid-twenties.

If the lesson did continue, Confucius's demands increased. Though most of his students initially came to him looking only for the means to obtain a government job, Confucius convinced them that their sights should

"If I uncover one corner and a student cannot discover the other three, I end the lesson."

be set much higher. He taught them about poetry and ritual, about music and history. He coaxed them into discussions of current events and debated them on issues of morality. But through all of these various lessons ran what Confucius called "a single thread." He wanted them to try, as he was trying, to follow in the footsteps of the Duke of Zhou. He wanted them to try to enter upon the Way.

JUNZI

To help his students (and himself) along, he held up an ideal of virtuous behavior called the junzi. Junzi, which literally means "son of a ruler," had previously been used only to describe members of the upper class. Confucius wanted his students to

This nineteenth-century painting shows Confucius and his students. Confucius taught his students that true greatness arose from their ethical thoughts and good deeds.

realize that true greatness in a person has nothing to do with what class they are born into and everything to do with their thoughts and their deeds. He changed the meaning of the word. A junzi became someone who held virtue above all else. A junzi was what he and all of his students strove to be.

"A junzi seeks the Way, he does not seek a living," said Confucius. "Plough the fields and perchance you may still go hungry. Apply yourself to learning and perchance you may yet make a career. A junzi worries whether he will find the Way; he does not worry that he may remain poor."

"A junzi worries whether he will find the Way; he does not worry that he may remain poor."

Such demands scared off almost everyone. Nearly the entire society was moving in one direction—toward selfish gain—and Confucius was proposing that his students move in the opposite direction. His disciples were few. "A man who can study for three years without giving a thought to his career is hard to find," he admitted. But Confucius did not compromise his vision. He continued to cut against the grain. It made for a life that had in it the potential for vast loneliness.

But Confucius did not go through life alone.

This woodcut shows Confucius playing a lute for his students. Zilu, Ran Qui, and Zigong were among the students who remained with Confucius for many years.

LOYAL FRIENDS

Among Confucius' earliest students was a man only a few years younger than him named Zilu. One passage in *The Analects* describes this man succinctly: "Zilu was wild." Zilu was brave to the point of being foolhardy. He was also stubborn, boastful, a slow but tenacious learner, and fiercely loyal. And he was Confucius' best friend.

As the two men grew up and then grew old together, they developed a relationship in which they considered each other as equals. Confucius always encouraged his disciples to challenge him in debate, but Zilu on several occasions went beyond this kind of philosophical challenge to take issue with his teacher on matters that would shape Confucius's life. And on more than one occasion Confucius veered from his original plan to follow the advice of his friend Zilu.

For his part, Confucius, in attempting always to steer his disciple along the Way, needled Zilu with the kind of barbs only the closest of friends can throw at each other. On one occasion, Confucius was praising the merits of another disciple. Zilu, fishing for praise on his own merits, asked, "If you had command of the army, whom would you take as your lieutenant?"

"For my lieutenant," said Confucius, pausing to fix his friend with a stare, "I would not choose a man who wrestles with tigers or swims across rivers without fearing death. He should be full of apprehension before going into action and always prefer a victory achieved by strategy." Though there was often a light tone in his words to Zilu, Confucius had genuine concern that the mixture of recklessness and unswerving loyalty in his friend would lead to a bad end in such a violent world. Thinking on this matter one day he mused, "A man like Zilu will never die a natural death."

Two other disciples who traveled through life with Confucius were Ran Qiu and Zigong. These two men were much closer to the average SHI of the day than either Confucius or Zilu. When they first came to Confucius they had dreams of purely personal success. But they also carried in them some small seed of goodness, some desire to investigate more deeply the world and their place in it. If they did not have this in them, Confucius would not have taken them on as students. He said, "If a person does not continually ask himself, 'What am I to do about this, what am I to do about this?' there is no possibility of my doing anything about them."

Confucius saw early on that the bright and opportunistic Ran Qiu possessed the ability to go far in politics. But the teacher worried that Ran Qiu would not carry a sense of higher purpose with him as he climbed upward through the government ranks. "It is not that I do not enjoy the Master's Way," Ran Qiu said at one point, "but I do not have the strength to follow it."

"He who does not have the strength can always give up halfway," Confucius replied. "But you have given up before starting."

Zigong, like Ran Qiu, had the kind of talents that went a long way in the world at that time. He was blessed with the gift of gab. Confucius saw that Zigong would be able to succeed, if he wanted to, just where Confucius had failed. He would be able to tell influential people just what they wanted to hear and tell it to them with style and pizzazz. Confucius, who quickly developed a soft spot in his heart for Zigong, saw that such talents would in the end lead only to an empty life.

> **"He who does not have the strength can always give up halfway, but you have given up before starting."**

Thinking of the kind of person who lives without any higher purpose, Confucius said, "A gentleman (junzi) is not a pot." A pot has no higher purpose. A pot has no dreams of improving the world. Like a person whose only hunger is for worldly success, a pot can only be filled.

Despite his failings, Zigong distinguished himself as a disciple of Confucius in two ways.

First of all, he displayed a loyalty to his teacher that would come in the end to rival that of Zilu's for its longevity and passion. And second, Zigong doggedly kept trying to understand his teacher's message, even though the message often seemed to him as unreachable as the moon. He once compared Confucius to a high-walled mansion, saying, "Few are those who are granted access!" Yet he kept trying to gain access, asking Confucius again and again about the junzi. Confucius, who always tailored his teaching to each individual disciple, told the garrulous Zigong that the junzi "preaches only what he practices."

Still, Zigong was not able to bring his deeds into accord with his words. He tried impressing Confucius once by parroting one of Confucius' favorite maxims, saying, "I would not want to do to others what I do not want them to do to me."

"Oh, you have not come that far yet!" Confucius replied. For Confucius, words had to come straight from the heart and, moreover, they had to be backed up by deeds. Otherwise they were meaningless.

ALL ARE WELCOME

Most of Confucius' disciples came, like Ran Qiu and Zigong, from the SHI class. But Confucius, once again cutting against the grain of his times, allowed students from any and every walk of life. Other tutors followed along in the prevailing belief that only those of so-called high birth could ever amount to anything. Coming from a peasant upbringing himself, Confucius knew that it was possible for anyone to set out upon the Way. "I never denied my teaching to anyone who sought it, even if he was too poor to offer anything more than a token present for his tuition," he said.

"I never denied my teaching to anyone who sought it."

Early in Confucius' teaching career, a poor and sickly peasant named Yan Hui came to him. Confucius did not turn him away. At first, Confucius did not know what to make of his new student. Yan Hui was so reluctant to open his mouth that it was difficult to tell if he was absorbing any of Confucius's teaching at all. But after watching closely for a while, Confucius saw the truth about the meek peasant. "I can talk all day to Yan Hui—he never raises any objection, he looks stupid," said Confucius. "Yet, observe him when he is on his own: his actions fully reflect what he learned. Oh no, Hui is not stupid."

"[H]is actions fully reflect what he learned."

In this illustration, Yan Hui follows his teacher Confucius. Over the years, the introspective Yan Hui emerged as Confucius's favorite student.

From his first days with Confucius, Yan Hui centered all his energy on learning. As fellow disciples like Zigong lost themselves in the clouds of their own fancy speech, Yan Hui struggled silently to find the Way that Confucius was forever pointing to.

"The more I contemplate it, the higher it is," said Yan Hui of Confucius' teaching. "The deeper I dig into it, the more it resists; I see it in front of me, and then suddenly it's behind me. Step by step the Master skillfully lures me on. He stimulates me with literature, he restrains me with ritual. Even if I wanted to stop, I could not. Just as all my resources are exhausted, the goal is towering above me; I long to embrace it, but cannot find the way."

A bond began to develop between the two men. Confucius saw in his disciple a kindred spirit. Yan Hui was the only person he ever came across who loved learning as much as he did. When he spoke of Yan Hui over the years, his voice became more and more lit up by an unmistakable note of awe. It seemed that nothing could prevent the often poverty-stricken disciple from his joyous attempts to walk upon the Way. "How admirable is Yan Hui!" said Confucius. "A handful of rice to eat, a gourd of water to drink, a hovel for a shelter—no one would endure such misery, yet Yan Hui's joy remains unaltered. How admirable is Yan Hui!"

Confucius believed that it was Yan Hui who came closer than anyone to embodying the virtues of the junzi, the perfect individual. One day as he sat talking with Zigong Confucius asked, "Which is better, you or Yan Hui?"

"How could I compare myself to Yan Hui?" asked Zigong. "From one thing he learns, he deduces ten; from one thing I learn, I only deduce two."

"Indeed, you are not his equal," said Confucius. "And neither am I."

CHAPTER FIVE

教师

THE OUTSIDER

As he approached 40 years of age, Confucius still hadn't found a job in government. He loomed large in the thoughts of his few disciples, but in Lu people considered him an oddity—or didn't consider him at all. Once, in an attempt to make his ideas known to those in power, he went to a dinner party for high-ranking officials at the Ji family home. He was met at the door by the Ji family steward, who said, "My lord has invited everyone of importance. He didn't invite you."

Confucius's status as a political outsider, in that instance, branded him as someone of no importance. Nevertheless, he continued to speak out against the corrupt practices of the three powerful families of Lu, and slowly Confucius became a nagging thorn in their side.

When Confucius saw something going wrong in the world, he did not keep silent. He heard of an excessively lavish ceremony at the Ji family ancestral temple. Previously, the ceremony had been one that only the Duke of Lu was allowed to perform. Confucius saw that the head of the Ji family was blatantly communicating the fact that he, and not the Duke, now ruled Lu. What troubled Confucius was that the head of the Ji family, unlike the Duke, didn't have to justify any "Mandate of Heaven." He didn't have to concern himself with the welfare of the people. He didn't have to concern himself with anything but the increase of his own power. "If he is capable of that," said Confucius of the head of the Ji family and his lavish ceremony, "what will he not be capable of?"

> **"If he is capable of that, what will he not be capable of?"**

That comment, and others like it, put Confucius in a perilous position when a violent disturbance broke out in Lu in 517 B.C. The puppet leader of Lu, Duke Chao, attempted at that time to seize the reins of power in his state by attacking the Ji family. The Meng and the Shu families rallied to the aid of the Ji family and Duke Chao's weak forces were routed. The Duke fled into exile. Confucius, surmising that the three families might be in the mood to snuff out the life of anyone who had spoken against them, followed the Duke out of Lu.

For several years, Confucius lived in the state of Qi. He supported himself there by continuing to teach. Also, he managed to gain an audience with the ruler of Qi, Duke Jing. Duke Jing and Confucius discussed political theory, and the Duke was impressed with the traveling scholar's thoughts. But Duke Jing, like many rulers whom Confucius would speak with in the future, neglected to put any of Confucius's ideas into action. They ruled with an eye toward personal gain, and they ruled by force. Confucius's ideas were to them like songs to enjoy and then, when it came time for the actual business of ruling, to put away.

While in Qi, Confucius heard a song that he would never put away. It was called the "Coronation Hymn of Shun," and it mesmerized Confucius from the moment its opening notes touched his ears. He drifted away from the ugliness and disappointments of his world. He drifted into the song itself, which told of the peaceful ascension to the throne of the ancient Xia dynasty ruler Shun. Another legendary emperor, Yao, had realized that Shun was more virtuous than he and had stepped down from the throne to let Shun become emperor. *The Analects* describes Confucius's reaction to the music: "For three months, he forgot the taste of meat." For three months he lived in the music, and the music lived in him. He said, "I never imagined that music could reach such a point."

RETURNING HOME

In or around 509 B.C., Confucius returned home. Lu had not changed much. The Ji family still ruled. Duke Ding (the younger brother of the exiled Duke Chao) served as the puppet leader. Some of Confucius's disciples had begun to find success in government service, but Confucius remained the quintessential outsider. He was not as willing as these disciples to compromise his beliefs, and his uncompromising nature did not go unchallenged.

> ### "All I am waiting for is the right offer."

"If you had a precious piece of jade," asked his disciple Zigong, "would you hide it safely in a box, or would you try to sell it for a good price?"

"I would sell it! I would sell it!" Confucius replied. "All I am waiting for is the right offer."

In 505 B.C. an offer came. Yang Huo, a high-ranking officer of the Ji family, had turned on his bosses, sparking a violent rebellion that enabled him to grab control of the family and, by extension, of Lu. He came to Confucius in hopes of convincing him to take office. Confucius detested violent rebellion, and he saw that a country led by a bandit would become a country of bandits. He did not take office with Yang Huo, but appears at

*Confucius, pictured here in an undated
painting, returned from Qi around 509 B.C.*

any rate to have been moved by some of Yang
Huo's words. He said to Confucius, "Can a man be
called virtuous if he keeps his talents for himself
while his country is going astray? I do not think
so. Can a man be called wise if he is eager to act,
yet misses every opportunity to do so? I do not

think so. The days and months go by. Time is not with us."

Confucius realized that he had been holding out for a perfect situation, and, because the world was far from perfect, that situation would never come.

By 502 B.C., Yang Huo had been defeated and had fled from Lu. But the Ji family continued to have problems with rebellious officers. In that year an officer named Gongshan Furao took over the Ji stronghold in Bi. He looked to Confucius for help. This time, Confucius was tempted. But his disciple Zilu vehemently opposed Confucius on this matter. "It is too bad if we have nowhere to go," he said, "but is this a reason to join Gongshan?" Confucius replied, "Since he is inviting me, it must be for some purpose."

"If only someone would employ me, I could establish a new Zhou Dynasty in the East."

Confucius momentarily blinded himself to the fact that his prospective boss was a violent, power-hungry rebel. He saw instead the possibility that Gongshan Furao had called upon him to be the architect of a more just and harmonious society.

In the end he did not go with Gongshan Furao. But his final words with Zilu on the subject reveal both the lofty purpose Confucius saw for himself and the budding frustration and even sadness over the fact that this purpose was not being realized. "If only someone would employ me," he said, "I could establish a new Zhou dynasty in the East."

A GOVERNMENT POSITION

In 501 B.C., Confucius finally took a job as an advisor to the Ji family, who had undoubtedly been moved to make their offer after watching two rebellious underlings vie for his services. They didn't want Confucius going against them, so they brought him into their own employ.

Inflated myths have come to cloud this period of Confucius' life. Sima Qian wrote in the first biography of Confucius that the Master was made the Grand Secretary of Justice and then promoted to the Chief Minister of State. And, according to this story, not only was Confucius given the power to run the state, but he ran it so well that he ushered in a brief period of utopian harmony for the corrupt and violent state of Lu. Qian wrote, "After three years of his premiereship . . . things lost on the street were not stolen, and foreigners visiting the country did not have to go to the police, but all came to Lu like a country of their own."

If Confucius had attained such high offices and such spectacular effects, it surely would have been mentioned in *The Analects*. It isn't. There are few mentions of him holding an office at all, and these imply that Confucius's level of influence was somewhere between low and none. The truth is that, after years and years of hoping for a chance to "build a new Zhou dynasty in the East," Confucius was given a job with a lofty title but almost no responsibilities. He was put in a place where his radical ideas would not have a chance of being heard. He was voiceless.

By the turn of the fifth century B.C., Confucius had decided to take his quest for a virtuous leader elsewhere. Mencius, writing at a time before overblown myths buried the facts of this part of the Master's life, wrote that Confucius decided to leave Lu because, simply, he was "not used."

CHAPTER SIX

教师

PURSUING THE IMPOSSIBLE

Confucius and his disciples crossed through the border guard's gate, leaving Lu for the state of Wei. The caravan soon came upon a mass of peasants on their way from one region to another. Ran Qiu asked Confucius, "Once the people are many, what next should be done?"

"Enrich them," Confucius replied.

"Once they are rich, what next should be done?"

"Educate them," Confucius answered. Confucius knew what he wanted to do. Whether he knew how he was going to do it is debatable. For sixteen years, Confucius and his disciples seemed to roam aimlessly through the states surrounding Lu. The events that occurred during these wandering years have no specific dates or order, but scholars agree that the wanderings began and ended in the state of Wei.

Not long after their arrival in Wei, Confucius

Confucius, depicted here in an undated engraving, was seized by Kuang villagers, who mistook him for a bandit. He and his students were eventually released.

realized that he was being followed. An agent of one of the factions battling for power in the state shadowed his every move. It was a not-so-gentle hint that Confucius and his radical ideas were wanted in Wei even less than they had been wanted in Lu.

Before he left Wei, Confucius had his hopes raised by an invitation from the duke to join him on a carriage ride. Confucius hurried to the imperial palace, only to get there and find that the duke's favorite concubine would be riding in the royal carriage and Confucius would be riding in a second carriage. He was then, in effect, paraded through the streets of Wei as a voiceless buffoon.

A CLOSE CALL

Things did not go any smoother upon leaving Wei. South of Wei, in a town along the border of Lu called Kuang, villagers mistook Confucius for a traveling bandit who had previously victimized their town. During a confused fracas, Yan Hui was separated from Confucius and the other disciples. Confucius and his remaining disciples were then thrown in jail.

Behind bars, Confucius thought only of his missing disciple. Days passed with no sign of Yan Hui. When finally the doors of the prison cell swung open and Yan Hui walked through, an overjoyed Confucius exclaimed, "I thought you were dead!" Yan Hui replied, "While you are alive how would I dare to die?"

In Kuang, Confucius refused to worry about his own safety, even when it seemed certain that his captors were going to execute him. He said to his despondent cellmates, "King Wen is dead; is civilization not resting on me now? If Heaven intends civilization to be destroyed, why was it vested in me? If Heaven does not intend civilization to be destroyed, what should I fear from the people of Kuang?"

Confucius believed that he had been put on Earth to keep alive the vision of a harmonious world. As it turned out, a man who had briefly studied under Confucius in Wei vouched for Confucius, and the people of Kuang let him go.

Later in his travels Confucius and his disciples wound up in the southern state of Song. A military official named Huan Ti, angered by Confucius' philosophy (which certainly ran counter to Huan Ti's violent ways) and by the fact that his own younger brother Sima Niu had become a disciple of Confucius, began to menace Confucius.

Mencius wrote that Confucius and the disciples dressed in "inconspicuous clothing" while in Song in an attempt to keep a low profile. Huan Ti, in a show of force, had the big tree that Confucius and the disciples had been meeting under uprooted.

Confucius realized that not only his life, but also the lives of his disciples were at risk and so he decided to once again move on. "We'd better hurry," one of his disciples told him. "Heaven vested me with moral power," Confucius replied. "What do I have to fear from Huan Ti?"

As they were leaving Song, Confucius got separated from his disciples. Confucius was wracked with worry over the fate of his friends. When they reunited, Zigong told Confucius that a townsman had spoken to them of "a man standing at the east gate with a brow like a hero and a neck the same. But from the waist down, he stands there as glum as a dog at a funeral."

> **"Heaven vested me with moral power."**

"I don't know about my heroic torso," Confucius said, "but the dog at the funeral, that fits, that fits!"

TAKING GREAT JOY IN LIFE

Confucius never lost his sense of humor, even when things looked grim. Nor did he lose his sense of joy. By all accounts, he lived during these years on the road a very humble existence, subsisting on whatever meager sums he could get as a sort of visiting lecturer. But this was not important to him: "With coarse food to eat, water to drink, and my bended arm for a pillow, I still have joy in the midst of these things."

He took great joy in continuing to learn more and more about the world as he traveled. He visited libraries wherever he went and, as always, learned from everyone and everything that he came in contact with. The disciples marveled at his ability to unlock the secrets of the world. Zigong said, "The Master obtains information by being cordial, kind, courteous, temperate, and deferential. The Master has a way of inquiring which is quite different from other people's, is it not?" He demanded nothing. He kept his eyes and ears open and, more important, he simply loved learning. And love has a way of opening up doors that have been locked.

Confucius was not without worries while out on the road. These worries had nothing to do with material comforts: "Failure to cultivate moral power, failure to explore what I have learned, incapacity to stand by what I know to be right, incapacity to reform what is not good—these are my worries."

This last worry, being unable to "reform what is not good," began to haunt Confucius. The more he traveled around China, the more he saw that the suffering, the immorality, and the chaos in Lu was present everywhere and that he seemed powerless to stop any of it. He had not set out on his quest to fail. He wanted a position at the side of a ruler.

In the state of Jin, Confucius was offered a job by a man named Bi Xi. Again this offer came not from someone whom Confucius would have considered a legitimate ruler but from an officer who seems to have had designs on violently seizing control of his state. Nonetheless, Confucius was tempted by the offer. But Zilu stood in his way. Just as he had when a similar offer had come for Confucius in Lu, Zilu raised questions about serving an immoral ruler.

Confucius replied to the questions by saying, "What resists grinding is truly strong, what resists black dye is truly white." He knew, however, that his friend was right. He did not in the end take the job. But the years of failure were beginning to wear on him. Confucius's final thoughts on the job offer came in the form of a question for his friend Zilu: "Am I just a bitter gourd, good only to hang as decoration but unfit to be eaten?"

> **"Am I just a bitter gourd, good only to hang as decoration but unfit to be eaten?"**

Not long after that, Zilu met up with a hermit who had retired from the world, believing that it was beyond saving. "Where are you from?" the hermit asked him. Zilu replied that he was from Confucius's household. "Oh," said the hermit, "is that the one who keeps pursuing what he knows is impossible?"

HARDSHIPS

Confucius and the disciples traveled to Chen, where their situation got worse than ever. Myths later arose about their hardships in Chen which painted Confucius as an important political figure caught in the crossfire of a raging war between two states. This did not happen. In *The Analects*, it says nothing of political problems, but only, "In Chen, supplies fell short." This suggests the humble reality that Confucius and his disciples were not being held prisoner by a huge army, as one popular tale had it, but rather that, after several years on the road, their meager way of barely scraping by was on the brink of failing them altogether. The passage in *The Analects* continues, "His followers became weak: they could no longer rise to their feet."

They were not caught up in any sort of grand political drama but were simply starving to death. They were not surrounded by armed guards but

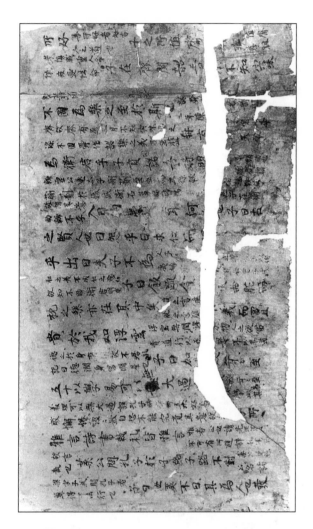

This is a page from a Tang dynasty manuscript of The Analects of Confucius *that was found in 1967. The Analects contain the sayings and anecdotes of Confucius.*

only by indifferent rocks and trees and the sky. Confucius was the only one not affected by the hunger and, more important, by the feeling that all their travels and all their efforts had been in vain.

"How is it possible," he asked, "for a gentleman to find himself in such distress?"

"A gentleman can indeed find himself in distress," Confucius replied. "But only a small man is swept off his feet by it."

Confucius and his disciples did manage to avoid starving to death. They traveled on toward the capital of Chen but, once there, were unable to gain an audience with the ruler. Confucius was beginning to feel the futility of his quest. He also started wondering whether his place was at home, in Lu, teaching youngsters and guiding his disciples who had become government ministers. "Let us go back, let us go back!" Confucius said. "Our young people are full of fire, they have brilliant talents, but they do not know yet how to use them."

Despite these words, Confucius did not return home. He and the disciples continued to drift from state

> **"Our young people are full of fire, they have brilliant talents, but they do not know yet how to use them."**

to state. In 484 B.C., Confucius wound up back in Wei. It appears that at this time he finally decided to accept a job offer from a government officer, Kong Yu, who had a less-than-glowing reputation. In later years Confucius defended this officer and his decision to work for him, saying that "he had an agile mind, was fond of learning, and was not ashamed to seek enlightenment from his inferiors."

The history books of that time paint Kong Yu in a different light, describing him as a typical officer of the times, generally concerned only with his own advancement. That Confucius ended up working under him shows how far short of his dream of serving at the side of a virtuous ruler he had fallen, and how desperate he had become to try to make the dream happen. He did not stay long with Kong Yu, realizing soon enough that his advice was only being sought to make Kong Yu more powerful. All his knowledge and ideas about how society could be improved were disregarded. When he told Kong Yu that he was going to leave, Kong Yu, perhaps displaying the qualities that Confucius would later laud him for, begged forgiveness from Confucius and promised that he would listen to him more in the future. Confucius was considering staying on with Kong Yu when messengers arrived from Lu.

RETURNING HOME

There are in this moment, as with many of the moments in Confucius' life, inflated myths obscuring the facts. One myth tells that the messengers came in a caravan of 80 golden chariots to spirit Confucius back home.

A more likely scenario is that Confucius, thanks to a recommendation from the now-successful Lu official Ran Qiu, was offered back his old, meaningless position with the government. Thinking about the "young people . . . full of fire," Confucius accepted the less-than-spectacular offer. He wanted to go home, and did so, and not in any convoy of 80 golden chariots. He went home the way he had left, riding beside one of his disciples in a creaking, one-horse carriage.

CHAPTER SEVEN

教师

PRIVATE WISHES

By the time he returned to Lu, Confucius was in his late sixties. An air of resignation, and even of sadness, had crept into his life.

"I am getting old," he said. "It has been a long time since I last saw in a dream the Duke of Zhou." Confucius's lifelong dream of becoming a latter-day Duke of Zhou had evaporated, but he didn't allow this to overwhelm him or to slow him in his efforts to bring the Way of the Duke of Zhou back into the world. He also didn't allow the loss of his dream to cause him to forget about joy.

Joy was to Confucius what the bulls-eye is to an archer. He needed only to focus on it to thrive. For Confucius, joy resided in learning, in improving himself, in teaching, and in simply reveling in the company of friends. "To learn something and then to put it into practice at the right time: is this not a joy? To have friends coming from afar:

As in this portrait, Confucius typically has been portrayed as an old man because age connotes wisdom.

is this not a delight?" Confucius then added in the same breath, "Not to be upset when one's merits are ignored: is this not the mark of a gentleman?"

By aiming at the target of these simple yet

"To learn something and then to put it into practice at the right time: is this not a joy?"

important joys and delights, Confucius could hone in on the Way. He could cast off thoughts of bitterness, anger, and envy that occasionally buzzed around the outskirts of his mind. He had by now seen countless men less qualified than him serving at high levels of government. That less-than-saintly thoughts occurred to Confucius over the years are evidenced by his own frank admissions of human frailty. "I make no claims to wisdom or to human perfection—how would I dare? Still," he continued, "my aim remains unflagging and I never tire of teaching people."

Confucius had come to realize that people were shaped by their hopes and dreams. He had seen the massive

"I make no claims to wisdom or to human perfection—how would I dare?

suffering caused by those whose only hopes and dreams were of material wealth, profit, fame, and power. And he had seen that his own dream of

Confucius taught his students at this spot, the Terrace of the Apricot Tree, at the Temple of Confucius in Cou.

becoming a latter-day Duke of Zhou—even though it had failed, even though it had at times brought him sorrow—had ultimately lifted his life into the realm of joy. He tried to pass this knowledge on.

One day he was sitting and talking with his two closest friends, Yan Hui and Zilu. When the threesome had first come together so many years before, their faces had been smooth as polished stone. Now they were old. Confucius looked at his friends and said, "Suppose you tell me your innermost wishes?"

Confucius knew both men inside and out. He knew their strengths and their shortcomings. But he wanted to hear from them exactly what they wanted out of life. He knew such a question would illicit an answer that would define the disciples. It would show exactly how far they had come along the Way, and how far they still had to travel.

The ever-brash Zilu was the first to answer. "I wish I could share my carriages, horses, clothes, and furs with my friends without being upset when they damage them."

"I wish," said Yan Hui, "I would never boast of my good qualities or call attention to my good deeds."

Both replies had in them noble aspirations. But they also had traces of what Confucius sometimes referred to as "the small person." Zilu showed with his wish a desire to put a higher value in his friends than in any material possessions, but also seemed to suggest that he, as the benevolent hero, was to be celebrated. Yan Hui's wish was one born from looking in the mirror rather than looking at the world. Both wishes were self-centered, despite their basically good intentions.

"I wish the old may enjoy peace, friends may enjoy trust, and the young may enjoy affection."

For a moment, no one spoke. Zilu broke the silence. "May we ask what are our Master's private wishes?"

Confucius said, "I wish the old may enjoy peace, friends may enjoy trust, and the young may enjoy affection."

CHAPTER EIGHT

教师

"HEAVEN IS DESTROYING ME"

In 481 B.C. a youthful heir to the throne in the state of Qi was murdered by an official intent on seizing power for himself. Confucius was appalled. He realized that if the murderous official went unchallenged, a similar act could occur closer to home. The Ji, Shu, and Meng families could easily be encouraged to do violence to Ai, now the Duke of Lu. And so Confucius, now 70 years old, once again donned the robes he had worn as an advisor in Lu. He was not yet done trying to change the world.

He went to Duke Ai hoping to convince him to send troops to Qi to overthrow the assassin. The Duke, aware of his status as a powerless puppet, replied weakly, "report to the Three Lords," meaning the heads of the Meng, Shu, and Ji families. Confucius did so, knowing beforehand that the three families would have absolutely no problem with the assassination of anyone, even a child. As *The Analects* put it, "They refused to intervene."

His visit to the three families would prove, fittingly, to be the last of Confucius' many fruitless attempts to directly influence political affairs. But, in other ways, he kept trying to bring the Way of the ancients to the world.

CONVERSATIONS WITH DUKE AI

Confucius continued to speak about politics with Duke Ai. These conversations, featuring on the one hand the philosopher who no one in power ever listened to, and on the other hand the ruler who had no power, would have been exercises in futility if not for one thing: the disciples were listening. They remembered Confucius's words and later committed them to paper. Confucius's political philosophy thus was allowed to survive after him. A little over a century later the great thinker Mencius would take up that philosophy and build it into something that would eventually bend the ears of rulers all over China. Confucius's political philosophy would change the world, though such a possibility would have struck him as ludicrous as he conversed with the powerless Duke in his crumbling royal castle.

On one occasion, Confucius said to Duke Ai, "Raise the straight and set them above the

CHINOIS CÉLÈBRES.
(Voyez tome Ier, pages 3o6 et 333.)
MENG-TSEU, PHILOSOPHE CHINOIS.

*Mencius (ca. 372–ca. 289 B.C.) was the preeminent
Confucian scholar, and his writing on
Confucius's thought are highly respected.*

crooked, and the hearts of the people will be won.
If you raise the crooked and set them above the
straight, the people will deny you their support."
Ever since first learning about the Duke of Zhou,
Confucius believed that the health of a society

was largely determined by the trust the people had in their political leaders.

GOOD GOVERNMENT

In conversations with his disciples who had become government officials, Confucius tried repeatedly to emphasize the importance of the people in all political equations. He told Zigong, now a successful official in Lu, "Without the trust of the people, no government can stand."

> **"Without the trust of the people, no government can stand."**

Confucius' most radical political thoughts came in his discussions with his disciples. To Ran Qiu, who had found more success as an official than any other disciple, Confucius made frequent and ardent pleas on behalf of those who previously had received little consideration. Political leaders seldom paid attention to the masses, and Ran Qiu was no exception. "If there is equality," Confucius told him, "there will be no poverty."

Confucius was often disappointed by his disciples who had a chance to make a difference, and by none so much as Ran Qiu. The long relationship between teacher and disciple eventually ended because of Ran Qiu's selfish political practices.

As it is put in *The Analects*, "The head of the Ji family was richer than a king, and yet Ran Qiu kept pressuring the peasants to make him richer still." Confucius's reply to this behavior was blunt and final. He said of Ran Qiu, "He is my disciple no more. Beat the drums, my little ones, and attack him: you have my permission."

MERIT SYSTEM

The most radical of all of Confucius's thoughts was one that he championed within the sanctuary of his own school. He believed that a person chosen as leader of a government should be chosen on the basis of merit alone. Outside his sanctuary this was never practiced. Only members of the upper classes ever got to be leaders. But Confucius wanted to make sure that his students heard a harmonious song amidst the brutal noise of the world.

He practiced what he preached with his own disciples, putting the peasant-born Yan Hui above all other students

"Oh, Yan Hui, if you were a ruler I would be your butler!"

in terms of individual merit. He saw that Yan Hui could have been a leader. At one point, after Yan Hui said something that truly pleased Confucius,

Confucius exclaimed, "Oh, Yan Hui, if you were a ruler I would be your butler!"

Confucius championed another virtuous disciple from the peasant class, Ran Yong, by saying that he "has in him the makings of a prince." The implication—that a peasant could (and should) become a ruler—struck the other disciples as so shocking that it was as if Confucius had told them that he had built a ship and was going to sail up to the moon. It simply was beyond the realm of thought, for all but Confucius, that the highest seats in government could be filled by anyone other than those with so-called royal bloodlines. To help his disciples see the light on this matter, Confucius compared Ran Yong to the offspring of a plow ox and wondered aloud if such an ox would be rejected by "the Spirits of the Hills and Rivers" if it were used in a sacrifice. Heaven, he was implying, did not distinguish among persons of different classes. Everyone could elevate themselves to a higher position by means of ability and education. This idea would eventually change the world.

THE LIGHT GROWS DIMMER

But for all his world-shaking thoughts and his tireless adherence to the Way, Confucius was, in his old age, mellowing. He seemed to like nothing

*This statue of Confucius is located in
New York City. Despite Confucius's
failures to get his message heard
during his lifetime, his teachings
have spread throughout the world.*

better than to sit with a group of disciples, listening to them talk about their hopes and dreams.

One day, he sat with them and encouraged them to voice their desires for the future. All but one of the disciples in attendance hastened to tell of their lofty, ambitious dreams. It soon became obvious that they were merely trying to top each other and impress their Master. They weren't speaking from their heart.

While the somewhat insincere dreams were being told, a young disciple named Dian sat off in a corner playing an instrument resembling a zither. He kept silent while the others spoke. Confucius asked him what his wish was.

"I am afraid my wish is not up to those of my three companions," he said.

"There is no harm in that! After all, each is simply confiding his personal aspirations," said Confucius.

The disciple put down his instrument. "In late spring, after the making of the spring clothes has been completed, together with five or six companions and six or seven boys, I would like to bathe in the river Yi, and then enjoy the breeze on the rain dance terrace, and go home singing."

"I am with you, Dian," said Confucius.

Life was gradually slipping from the Master's grasp. He saw that he would never attain any measure of the success he had dreamed about.

Mentioning the two omens that would have announced the presence of a sage in the world, Confucius said, "The Phoenix does not come, the River brings forth no chart. It is all over for me!"

But more heartbreaking for Confucius than his personal failure was that as he neared the end of his own life he witnessed the end of the lives of many of the people closest to him. First his son, Bo yu, died. Then came the death of Confucius's kindred soul.

Yan Hui had once said to Confucius that he would not dare leave the earth so long as his Master lived, but in the end he was unable to honor these words. He died. Confucius wept wildly and raged at the stars. His disciples were shocked at the eruption of emotion on their Master's part. They had learned from Confucius himself about how ritualistic behavior should be used to keep emotional outbursts in check and to keep a person balanced. But Confucius was unbalanced.

"Heaven is destroying me!" he roared. "Heaven is destroying me!"

The disciples were alarmed that their Master was going beyond the normal behavior of a mourner. He seemed to them to be acting uncivilized, like a barbarian. "Master," a disciple said, "such grief is not proper."

"Heaven is destroying me!"

Confucius looked at the disciple. "If I did not grieve for Yan Hui," he asked, "for whom should I grieve?"

Not long after, Confucius became deathly ill. Zilu came and asked if he could pray for him. Confucius replied that he had already done all his praying. "What justifies me in the eyes of Heaven is the life I have led," he said.

His vision was clear until the end. He never lost himself in any delusions of grandeur. When Confucius was so sick that his disciples seemed sure that he would die, they came to his bedside as he slept. They had dressed themselves in lavish ceremonial garments that suggested they were high ministers attending the funeral of a king. They wished to obliterate the fact that Confucius had never received the high office that he had both wanted and deserved. Confucius awakened and looked around at his disciples in their fine garments and immediately realized what was going on.

"Who do you think I am going to deceive?" he asked. "Am I going to deceive Heaven?"

He then added quietly, "Besides, isn't it better to die with you, my friends, than with a whole lot of ministers?"

He recovered from this illness and lived on to see another sad day. Some time earlier, Zilu had gone off to serve a governor in the state of Wei. A violent rebellion broke out, and the rebels seemed to be on the brink of overrunning the government stronghold under Zilu's command. Other ministers decided to run for their lives. One of these ministers asked Zilu why he wasn't coming with them. "I have eaten their pay," Zilu said, referring to the noble family that employed him, "and will not now run from their misfortune." As the other minister ran, Zilu went to meet the swarming rebels with his sword drawn. He died fighting.

This stone stele was erected at the tomb of Confucius in 1443.

CHAPTER NINE

教师

MORE ESSENTIAL THAN WATER OR FIRE

Zigong was still alive. He came to see Confucius. "No one understands me," the old man said.

"Why is it that no one understands you?"

"I do not accuse Heaven, nor do I blame men," said Confucius. "Here below I am learning, and there above I am being heard. If I am understood, it must be by Heaven."

In 479 B.C., Confucius died. Mention of his final days is absent from *The Analects*. It is impossible to know just how Confucius left the world. Perhaps he died while surrounded by his friends, as he had wished.

Confucius's disciples spent the following three years in mourning. There is no mention, in the three years following the Master's death, of any of the disciples in the official record books of the time. It is a conspicuous absence, considering the fact that there was ample mention of the high-ranking officials who had studied under Confucius both before and after that period. Even Ran Qiu walked away from the political world for three years to grieve for Confucius. Zigong mourned for six.

Such devotion guaranteed that the sound of Heaven's wooden bell would echo through the world after Confucius' death. Confucius lived on through his disciples, who became teachers, and then as their own disciples became teachers. The loose array of sayings and anecdotes left behind in the memories of Confucius's disciples gradually shaped itself into a more systematic philosophy. Confucianism was born.

Confucius had once said, "Man can enlarge the Way. It is not the Way that enlarges man." The same came to be true of his teachings. Over the years they were enlarged. The greatest of all Confucianists was Mencius (372–289 B.C.), who developed Confucius's radical political ideas, declaring that the people had the right to overthrow an unjust ruler.

Mencius also echoed Confucius's belief that government officials' duties included speaking out against their ruler when the ruler's policies veered from the Way. In 213 B.C., hundreds of Confucianists paid with their lives for speaking out. They spoke out against the exceedingly harsh rule of the new Qin dynasty ruler, Shi Huangdi, who lashed out at the criticism by burying 400 Confucian scholars alive and by burning as many Confucian books as he could find.

A NEW DYNASTY

Shi Huangdi's despotic methods backfired and within 15 years his dynasty was overthrown. As the Qin dynasty ended and the Han dynasty began, Confucianists found themselves for the first time on the right side of a political struggle. Liu Bang, the first Han ruler, brought the Confucianists into his government, and a subsequent Han ruler, Wu Di, in 136 B.C. elevated Confucianism to the rank of the official religion of China. Wu Di also set up an examination system for prospective government officials. The examinations helped ensure that a person's rank in government was determined by merit and not by social standing.

As the years went by in China the Confucianists gained more and more power. Confucius's singular voice began to get lost in a philosophy that became increasingly rigid and rule-oriented. Policies were instituted in the name of Confucianism that would have made the old Master weep. In 841 A.D., a high-ranking Confucian official spearheaded a campaign to attack the two schools of thought that rivaled Confucianism in China, Buddhism and Daoism. Nearly five thousand monasteries were seized by the state, and about forty thousand shrines were destroyed. Confucius would have found particularly repugnant the fact that the Confucian official ordered that all Buddhist and Daoist books be burned.

CONFUCIUS LIVES ON

In the Song dynasty (960–1279 A.D.) Confucianism went through a further transformation. Philosophers who would later become known as Neo-Confucianists began further developing Confucius's thoughts on a concept called, in Chinese, li. Li (usually translated as principle or as a rite or a ceremony) was something that Confucius had constantly affirmed the importance of in both his teaching and his life.

For Confucius, li was the glue that held the world together. On a large scale, it was a royal ceremony that reaffirmed the Heaven-forged bond between a ruler and the people. On a smaller scale, it was a handshake that reaffirmed the bond between friends. In his view, the most important factor in any of these rituals was that they be performed with sincere feeling. He never elaborated on the specific components of any particular ritual. He knew that would have been like trying to tell someone how to make a handshake meaningful by describing exactly how much pressure the fingers should exert. The Neo-Confucianists shifted the focus on li from genuine feeling to details and guidelines. They elaborated and elaborated. Among the works produced by this school of thought was a manual for everyday behavior.

HEAVEN'S BELL

By the late 1800s, the thoughts of Confucius had traveled the world over. He truly had been Heaven's bell. Forms of Confucianism had been woven into the very fabric of life not only in China but also in Korea, Vietnam, and Japan. The thoughts of Confucius had begun to spread West as well. At

On September 28, 1990, students perform a traditional dance during a ceremony in Taipei, Taiwan, to mark Confucius's 2,540th birthday.

one and the same time Confucius spoke to a peasant farmer in rural China and to a reclusive philosopher in Massachusetts named Henry David Thoreau.

But by this time the official, state-sponsored Confucianism of China had stagnated. The government service examinations no longer tested merit and wisdom but only whether or not a person could memorize facts. The tests penalized any creativity. The final comment on this kind of Confucianism was that the ever-creative Confucius would undoubtedly have failed such an examination.

THE CULTURAL REVOLUTION

During the latter half of the nineteenth century, China became overrun with foreign invaders. First the British, and then the French, and finally the Japanese encroached on its previously unchallenged empire. The Chinese started to wonder why they were so weak when compared with their foes. Confucianism began to be seen as part of a past that seemed to weigh China down like a heavy layer of dead skin.

In 1949, Mao Zedong led the Communist party into power in China. He signaled that he would attempt to cast off the ways of the past, and Confucian thought in particular, when he said, "I

In this propaganda poster, students give Chairman Mao Zedong a report on food harvests. During the Cultural Revolution of the 1960s, the Communist government attempted to stamp out many Chinese traditions, including Confucianism.

hated Confucius from the age of eight." Mao's attack on the past reached its ugly climax in the Cultural Revolution of the 1960s. Young members of the Communist party known as Red Guards roamed the land in lawless, wolf-like packs. They burned books, humiliated and tortured scholars and teachers, and smashed whatever traces of China's long and illustrious past they came across. In the Shandong Province town of Qufu, Confucius' tomb monument was leveled by the

Red Guards. After the Red Guards had left, the people of the village gathered the broken stones of the monument and hid them away in their homes. When the Cultural Revolution finally ended, the stones were taken out of hiding and the monument was rebuilt.

"I hated Confucius from the age of eight."
—Mao Zedong

Mao also sought to instill in the people a belief that their strongest allegiance should be to their state and not to their family. His efforts failed, even with the Communist Party forcibly severing countless families by relocating family members to different places during the Cultural Revolution.

The Confucian emphasis on the importance of family remains today the primary strength of Chinese communities. In these communities, the norm is for family members to work together and sacrifice for one another. This familial cohesiveness has allowed Chinese immigrant communities to thrive throughout the world. In China, the strength of the family has helped temper the worst excesses of the communist regime. During times like the Cultural Revolution, the family offered a measure of humanity, a measure of kindness, in a world that had otherwise gone insane.

Confucius knew the power of a measure of humanity, and he knew its importance. "Humanity

A Chinese family in the Hubei province poses.
Confucius's emphasis on the importance of the
family remains an important force in China and
Chinese communities throughout the world.

"Humanity is more essential to people than water and fire."

is more essential to people than water and fire." He saw that being a good family member had the power to bring more humanity into the world. At times when the government has strayed far from the harmonious Way of the ancients—as in the Cultural Revolution—being a good family member became a political act, an act of quiet defiance.

Confucius also saw that there would be times when acts of not-so-quiet defiance were needed. "Tell the ruler the truth," he once said, "even if it offends him." This belief also sank roots deep into the Chinese soil.

In 1989, Chinese students, galvanized by the collapse of communism in the former Soviet Union, staged a massive protest in China's capitol city, Beijing. The peaceful protest went on for weeks, capturing the attention of the world. At one point the number of protesters in Beijing's Tiananmen square reached one million. As the protest endured, the student leaders' criticisms of the government and demands for more democracy became increasingly strident. After seven weeks of truth, the rulers had had enough. Army battalions were sent into Tiananmen Square. The protest ended in a bloodbath.

In June 1989, a man faces down a column of tanks during pro-democracy demonstrations in Beijing.

There is an image, caught on film, from the early stages of the massacre. The photograph shows a long line of army tanks on one of Beijing's wide boulevards. The army tanks had been advancing, but they are now frozen in their tracks—by a single man, standing with his arms at his sides.

"There are instances," Confucius said, "when righteous people will give their lives in order to fulfill their humanity."

551 B.C. Confucius is born Kong Qiu Zhing-Ni in Zou, Lou

549 B.C. Confucius's father, Shuleang He, dies

536 B.C. Confucius begins his formal education

532-25 B.C. Confucius's mother, Chengzai dies. Confucius gets a job with the Ji family as keeper of grain. He marries and has a son, Boyu. Confucius begins tutoring boys to get jobs as government officials.

517 B.C. Ji, Meng, and Shu families rout Duke Chao and Confucius is forced into exile

509 B.C. Confucius returns to Lu

505 B.C. Confucius refuses to serve as an advisor to corrupt rebel leader Yang Huo

502 B.C. Yang Huo is overthrown and Confucius refuses the place of advisor to his successor, Gongshan Furao

501 B.C. The Ji family gives Confucius a ceremonial job as advisor to the family

500 B.C. Confucius leaves for Wei and searches the states around Lu for an uncorrupted leader to serve

500–484 B.C. Kuang townspeople mistake Confucius for a bandit and jail him. In Song, military leader Huan Ti menaces Confucius for his radical beliefs. Confucius refuses a job offer in Jin and nearly starves to death with his followers in Chen.

484 B.C. Confucius accepts a job as advisor to Kong Yu but quits and returns to Lu

484–479 B.C. Confucius attempts to convince Ji, Meng, and Shu families to send troops to squelch a violent uprising in Qi. He discusses political philosophy with Duke Ai, puppet leader of Lu. Boyu, Confucius's son, and followers Yan Hui and Zilu die.

479 B.C. Confucius dies in Lu

136 B.C. Confucianism is elevated to the rank of official religion in China

A NOTE ON CHINESE SPELLING

Up until 1979, all the books written on Confucius in English utilized the Wade-Giles form of spelling Chinese words. That year, the press agency of the People's Republic of China devised a new system called Pinyin. In this book, Pinyin has been used to spell Chinese proper nouns, except in cases where the Wade-Giles form has become well-known—Confucius being the most prominent example.

The following is a list of the Pinyin words used in this book and their Wade-Giles equivalents.

Pinyin	*Wade-Giles*
Boyu	Po Yu
Daoism	Taoism
Gongshang Furao	Kung-Shan Fu-Jo
Junzi	Chung-tzu
Kong Shuleang He	Kong Shu-liang Ho
Mao Zedong	Mao Tse-tung

Ran Qiu	Jan Ch'iu
Sima Qian	Sse-Ma Ch'ien
Yan Chengzai	Yen Cheng-Tsai
Yan Hui	Yen Hui
Yang Huo	Yang Hu
Zigong	Tze Kung
Zilu	Tze Lu

A NOTE ON SOURCES

Confucius did not leave any writings behind. Researchers wishing to determine the actual facts of his life have to carve their way through the dense tangle of myths and legends that arose in the centuries following his death. By the time the first biography of Confucius was written—six centuries after his death by Sima Qian—the inflated view of the master's success in government had come to be seen as fact. The most reliable source of information about the life and teachings of Confucius comes from *The Analects,* which are sayings and anecdotes collected by Confucius's disciples. H.G. Creel, in his 1949 book, *Confucius: The Man and the Myth,* painted a clear picture of the master by supplementing an intense scrutiny of *The Analects* with a perusal of historical documents of the time, chiefly the *Spring and Autumn Annals.* Also, Creel gleaned information from the writings from the great Confucian scholar Mencius, who lived at a time—three hundred years after Confucius's death—before the legends and myths had obscured the facts of Confucius's life. Since Creel's book, there have been no ground-breaking biographies written, although in 1997, Simon Leys published a translation of *The Analects* which, on the strength of its extensive notes, emphasizes the humble facts of Confucius's life while elegantly underscoring the wisdom of his teachings.

FOR FURTHER READING

Chan, Wang-Tsit. *A Source Book in Chinese Philosophy*. Princeton, N.J.: Princeton University Press, 1963.

Cotterell, Arthur. *China: A Cultural History*. New York: Signet, 1988.

Creel, H. G. *Chinese Thought from Confucius to Mao Tse-tung*. Chicago: University of Chicago Press, 1953.

Creel, H. G. *Confucius: The Man and the Myth*. New York: John Day, 1949.

Hoobler, Dorothy, and Thomas Hoobler. *Confucianism*. New York: Facts on File, 1993.

Kinkead, Gwen. *Chinatown: Portrait of a Closed Society.* New York: HarperCollins, 1991.

Kelen, Betty. *Confucius: In Life and Legend.* New York: Nelson, 1972.

Leys, Simon, trans. *The Analects of Confucius.* New York: Norton, 1997.

Shimomura, Kojin. *A Book of Heaven and Earth.* Tokyo: University of Tokyo Press, 1973.

Smith, D. Howard. *Confucius.* New York: Scribner's, 1973.

Yutang, Lin, ed. *The Wisdom of Confucius.* New York: Random House, 1938.

http://www.west.net:80/~beck/
This award-winning site maintained by philosophy professor Sanderson Beck provides information about Confucius and other philosophers.

http://mars.superlink.net/user/fsu/
This site organizes many of the resources on Chinese philosophy that can be found on the Internet.

INDEX

ABOUT THE AUTHOR

Josh Wilker is the author of several young adult books, including a biography of Julius Erving and a history of classic cons and swindles. In 1989, he studied in China at the Shanghai Foreign Language Institute. Since then he has occasionally lectured on Chinese culture at the James Gutterson Cotter Society of East Asian Studies. He currently lives in Brooklyn, N.Y.